HOW YOUR
BOOK
SELLS
ITSELF

**10 Ways Your Book is Your
Ultimate Marketing Tool**

For information contact :

Bethany Atazadeh: bethanyatazadeh@yahoo.com

Mandi Lynn: mandi@stoneridgebooks.com

Cover Design by Stone Ridge Books

Formatting by Bethany Atazadeh

ISBN: 9781798430354 (paperback)

First Edition: March 2019

10 9 8 7 6 5 4 3 2 1

HOW YOUR BOOK SELLS ITSELF

10 Ways Your Book is Your Ultimate Marketing Tool

BETHANY ATAZADEH

WITH MANDI LYNN

CONTENTS

CHAPTER 1:
INTRODUCTION TO THIS SERIES

"Our job as marketers [is] to understand how the customer wants to buy and help them do so."
—Bryan Eisenberg

YOU'RE HERE BECAUSE you either published a book already—or you want to, very soon.

I've been in your shoes… it feels like you've sold exactly half a book in a million years, and you're wondering why you spent five thousand hours crafting this enormous masterpiece into absolute perfection... when no one cares.

So before we go anywhere near marketing, I need to say this to you: YOUR BOOK IS VALUABLE.

I'm going to have you read that over and over until you believe it, okay?

If we're going to do this thing together, I NEED you to believe in yourself—in those beautiful words you organized in pretty little rows on that creamy, yummy smelling page. You did that.

YOU.

That's more than most people will ever accomplish, and you should be extremely proud of yourself.

The first thing that will drastically change your marketing strategies and ability to sell books actually lies within that belief that **your writing is worth reading.**

You need to be excited about your book before anyone else will be!

But the reason you and I are here hanging out is because we need other people to be equally enthusiastic.

Mandi and I decided to write this series of books on *Marketing for Authors*, because we understand where you're coming from.

We know how it feels to love your work but not know how to spread the word.

If you want to know more about us, we'll include an "about the authors" section at the back, but for now, let's dive right into the good stuff:

When you break it down, BOOK SALES come from THREE THINGS:
1) Word of Mouth
2) Searches
3) Reviews

There are a billion different *methods*, but they all fall into one of these three categories. Either people are hearing about it from a friend or online source, or they're going out and actively looking for a book and stumble upon yours.

So it stands to reason that GOOD MARKETING means:

1) Getting people talking about your book and excited about it
2) Making your book searchable and easy to find
3) Getting lots and lots of book reviews (which is really just a specific form of word of mouth)

Again, there are a billion and one "methods" to selling books. Just a few examples are:

- Social media (such as Facebook, Instagram, Twitter, etc.)
- Websites
- Newsletters / Email Marketing
- Paid advertising
- Free advertising

- Influencers
- Street teams
- Reviews
- Advanced Reader Copies
- Blog tours
- Using search engines like Pinterest and YouTube
- Giveaways
- Guest posting
- Public speaking
- Conferences
- Press kits
- Newspaper and other media appearances
- And of course, utilizing features in the book itself. (Hint: the most important of all these tools!)

Feeling overwhelmed yet? Don't worry, that's why we're here to help you! We're going to talk about ALL those things in this series.

But just a reminder before we do, these are just "methods" or "tools" that lead to the three things I mentioned above: word of mouth, searches, and reviews.

Have you ever heard of "reverse engineering?"

Reverse engineering basically means figuring out your ultimate end goal or desired result, and then working your way backward from there to figure out how to get it.

Keeping the above three categories (word of mouth, searches, and reviews) in mind as our end goal, we will approach each of the different marketing methods out there and help you decide what will be most effective for YOUR book.

Because when it comes to methods, truthfully, learning how to market is often extreme trial and error. But that's where Mandi and I (Bethany) come in. You get to benefit from our personal trials and errors, our learning curves, and our "oops" moments, so that you don't have to deal with them. Instead you get to skip right over them and jump directly to the success!

How this book will work:

I see this book as the three of us sitting down in a cute little coffee shop and having a chat. I'll gush about all the exciting opportunities out there for your book, and ask you questions to help you figure out the best marketing method for YOUR story.

What this series will do for you:

Everyone reading this book will find that different methods work better for them than others. Mandi and I are going to dive into dozens of different marketing tactics. We'll share with you what worked well for us AND what didn't!

As we talk, I'll encourage you to pick your top three marketing strategies—I'll go into detail later in this book on why that's so important.

My focus has always been on how to advertise for free and save money wherever possible. Because let's be real, authors often don't make that much money in the beginning of their career. So why would you spend the little that you earn if you don't have to? You want to *make* money, not just break even, or worse, be in the red.

My goal in this series is to show you where you can spend your *time* instead of money, and secondly, how to waste less time, to ultimately help your books sell better and make you more money.

That said, we will still make sure to talk about different paid advertising options in this series as well, and our personal experiences with those. By the time we reach the end of the marketing series, we hope to cover every possible book marketing tool available to you and arm you with the knowledge and resources to choose the best tools to market YOUR books.

What this series is not:

This is not a "writing advice" or "self publishing advice" book, as much as we'd LOVE to talk about those topics (and could for hours)… we just don't have the time or space for that.

If you're interested in those topics and want to learn more from Mandi and I outside of this book, I'd encourage you to check out the back of the book where we list different resources and opportunities we provide for authors!

Both of us adore helping other authors to write and publish their books, so please take a look at that if you want to know more, but again, that's not the point of this book or this series. The point of this series is to help you SELL YOUR BOOK.

In this first book:

Like I mentioned, Mandi and I have a series planned where we will cover a vast number of marketing tools and resources, sharing our experience with each of them, offering recommendations and advice.

But in THIS book, I'm going to get extremely focused on what I truly believe is the NUMBER ONE MARKETING TOOL in helping you sell your book:

THE BOOK ITSELF.

We're about to talk about some marketing tips that blew my mind and changed everything for me.

Book sales have changed drastically. I can't emphasize enough how important it is to start by making sure your book is primed to sell itself.

But before we do that, we need to talk about why it matters…

CHAPTER 2:
WHY YOUR BOOK MATTERS

"The best way to predict the future is to create it."
–Peter Drucker

WE SPEAK FROM experience and our own mistakes when we say that your book truly is your most valuable marketing tool.

I doubt that comes as a surprise to you at this point, especially considering the title of this book, but I honestly can't overestimate *enough* just how much your book matters. The cover design, the title, the tagline, the back blurb, the formatting, the editing, and everything else that makes your book a book can have a powerful impact on sales, both negative and positive. A book done well can truly market itself.

This took me about six months after publishing to finally understand. I remember doing a ton of research on how to sell books better. I studied techniques and tips from other talented, self-published authors who were selling thousands of books.

And I've found that there are ten specific areas to focus on getting **right** for the book itself that could generate more sales than you'd ever expect, without having to lift a finger or press another repetitive ad campaign button. Not only that, but getting these ten things **wrong** will deter sales like nothing else.

Just to reinforce why we feel so strongly about this topic, Mandi and I wanted to take a second to share a few stories from our own experience, to better show you why we believe this is *so* vital to your book's success.

Bethany's Experience:

When I published my debut novel, *Evalene's Number* in 2017, I was playing a guessing game and hoping I was choosing right.

I remember watching YouTube video after YouTube video, taking notes, trying to understand each step of the publishing process.

There are a lot of great resources out there about the topics we're going to focus on in this book, and I'd definitely encourage you to do your own research to soak up as much knowledge as possible.

But no one told me just how important these ten things about the book itself would be for sales.

I had no clue that a cover could make or break a sale when I asked one of my good friends to help me design a simple cover. I had no understanding that a title could help with searchability. And I definitely didn't know how to format the book to help it fit genre expectations.

In the six months after publishing, my eyes were slowly opened to the fact that my book wasn't set in stone.

If it wasn't selling well, I could fix it!

Even in traditional publishing, I started noticing books would receive new covers and tag lines and formatting and so on. It made me take a closer look at my debut novel, and during that same time, I was working with my cover designer for the sequel in the series, *Pearl's Number*. I ended up asking them if they would also redesign the cover for the first book and rebrand the series as a whole.

Now my sales are drastically different from when I first began. No longer is it just friends who buy my book, but strangers too. Because the cover draws them in. Same thing applies to a good title, blurb, keywords, and so on.

I only wish I'd known this from the start. To be honest, I think I shot myself in the foot because if I'd taken the time to create the right cover the first time around, all those sales from family and friends plus strangers could have boosted me much further up in Amazon rankings (leading to a lot more sales).

I learned everything in this book the hard way, but that's why I'm *so* passionate about helping you with your book, because I want you to be able to learn from my mistakes!

Mandi's Experience:

I published my debut novel when I was seventeen, which means I didn't have everything quite figured out yet, but age in consideration, it came out pretty well!

In 2018, I did go into a re-branding phase after publishing my third novel, She's Not Here. *I had designed the first two covers of my books myself, but when it came to my third novel I wanted to bring in someone else to design it, and the result was gorgeous!*

On the downside, my old covers looked terrible in comparison. After a few months of consideration, I made the decision to rebrand and re-publish the first two novels. Originally the books had been published under free ISBN's so the new covers were a great opportunity to make the transition.

When re-publishing Essence, *the only changes that were made were to the cover and small formatting changes to fit my new branding. The cover was changed to fit the mood of the novel a bit better and to also give it a fresh look.*

I am Mercy *had a little more of a makeover. I reformatted the book in order to reduce the number of pages. The original copy of the book was so thick that it was more expensive to print than* Essence. *By making small changes to the formatting, I was able to reduce the book by about 100 pages.*

The next big change was in how I marketed the novel. I am Mercy *is considered a companion novel to* Essence, *meaning it's set in the same world as* Essence, *but has different characters.* Essence *is a young adult fantasy and initially I had marketed* I am Mercy *as an adult historical fantasy. But here's the thing: the main character of the book is about twenty years old. That meant it was in the weird limbo were the genre could go in either direction, young adult or adult. There were no overly dark elements of the novel to make it considered adult, so when I republished I changed the genre to young adult historical fantasy. This makes more sense when* Essence *is its companion novel and it will also perform better in its niche on Amazon because it's a very specific genre. We'll talk about this more later.*

I also changed the back-cover blurb for the book to get to the point much sooner to help hook in readers. Basically, all I did was delete one sentence.

The final touch was, of course, changing the cover to something that was not only eye-catching, but made you want to pick up the book and start reading to discover the story within.

After the re-publishing and re-branding, all books were published with ISBN's I purchased using my company, Stone Ridge Books, and all the covers used the same font where my name was listed on the front.

Why was all this rebranding a good thing? Because I was able to take books that had been published for years and give them new life!

A typical book has a shelf life of about two years. My books had been out for five and three years. They had long passed their shelf life and by re-publishing them I was able to reactivate excitement for them and see sales numbers I hadn't seen in years.

Was the re-publishing process stressful? I might go as far as saying re-publishing is more stressful than the initial publishing process. Did it cost money? You bet! Pretty covers aren't cheap! Was it worth it? Definitely.

Now I'm proud to display my new books alongside my first two novels because they are all gorgeous. Let's face it, people do judge a book by it's cover.

What Did We Learn?

Both Mandi and I learned the hard way just how important it is to get the book itself right.

We want to help YOU skip over that learning curve and all the hard lessons, by explaining to you everything we've learned along the way.

Like we say on the cover, the book itself can be your ultimate marketing tool.

Before we dive into the focus of THIS book and help you design the best book possible, we wanted to quickly break down these tools into different categories so you could see where this series is going.

In *Marketing for Authors*, we want to cover the following topics:

THE BOOK ITSELF: your genre, cover, title, back blurb, taglines/promotional lines, formatting, editing, keywords, categories, and your marketing mentality, as well as choosing the right marketing tools for you.

SOCIAL MEDIA MARKETING: on Instagram, Facebook, Twitter, Tumblr, SnapChat, etc.

SEARCH ENGINES: Pinterest, YouTube, Google, etc.

WEBSITES: your author website, your book's website, and other business sites.

EMAIL LISTS: newsletters with daily, weekly, or monthly content, whether author life focused or how to/help content focused, etc.

ACTIVITIES: giveaways, collaborations, book signings, author events, live book release parties, etc.

PAID ADVERTISEMENTS: such as Facebook Ads, Instagram Ads, Amazon Ads, etc.

REVIEWS: on Amazon, on Goodreads, requesting them from bookstagrammers or booktube or blogs, etc.

OTHER: book launches, post-book launch, choosing a publishing date, release week promotion, internet links, blog tours/vlog tours, promotional discounts, your own blog/vlog, book trailers, etc.

Everything on this list is optional... except THE BOOK ITSELF.

Yeah, it's true that social media can play a HUGE role in your online presence and book sales. Same goes for having a website as a central "hub" for all your information, or an email list to regularly keep your readers updated on new books you've written. But there ARE authors out there who don't have these things and they still sell books! Crazy right?

On the other hand, I don't know any authors who consistently sell a lot of books, if they don't have a quality book to sell.

It's important to note that traditional publishing houses handle some of the factors we're going to discuss in this book, but the majority of traditionally published authors are expected to also market their books themselves. This means developing a marketing mindset, which we'll talk about in detail. Even if you're reading this as a traditionally published author who has less control over things like the cover or the back blurb or keywords, it can still be helpful for you to know if your book has been set up for success by your publishing house.

When it comes to self-publishing, you have full control over your book. While we still highly recommend a social media presence, a website, and a newsletter, among other things, when it comes down to it, the *only* thing on this list that I personally believe is absolutely vital to selling books is **the book itself.**

It may seem like saying the sky is blue, but your book is your best marketing tool because:

- People judge books by their cover

- They will put a book down if the blurb or title doesn't catch their attention
- They're looking for books that remind them of other books they like
- They're looking for books that hook their attention
- They're looking for books in certain places
- They're looking for books that people are excited about—including the author

This is why you can't rush the process of creating a quality book. So many people just focus on the writing and think that if they do this, everything else will fall into place. The rest of the book—what it looks like, where it can be found, how it draws readers in—is often overlooked.

The truth is, you could write a masterpiece, but if you're hiding it under a rock, no one will ever know.

In the next chapter, we're going to go over ten different aspects of your book that you can focus on to help your book sell itself most effectively.

We're going to help you take your masterpiece and let the world know it exists.

CHAPTER 3:
HOW YOUR BOOK
SELLS ITSELF

"You have to tell a story, before you can sell a story."
—Beth Comstock

YOUR BOOK SELLS itself—OR *doesn't* sell itself—in ten specific ways. We're going to spend some time talking about each one of them in depth, asking you specific questions to see if you are using each of these aspects of your book to their fullest potential, but let's start by taking a look at all ten of them together:

1) The Genre
2) The Cover
3) The Title
4) The Back Blurb / Synopsis
5) The Tagline / Extra Promotional Lines
6) Interior Formatting
7) Editing
8) Keywords
9) Categories
10) And YOU as the author (your marketing mindset)

Each of these things can make or break book sales.

Sound dramatic? It's true. I'm coming to you from personal experience. When I published *Evalene's Number*, I learned many of these things the hard way.

The genre is often overlooked, but is actually one of the MOST important aspects of sales. For example, I chose to write dystopian with a Christian influence which is basically a genre mash-up… meaning there's no place on the virtual shelf! How do readers find your book if it's not in a genre they're already searching for? More importantly, can they even find it at all? More on genres in chapter 4.

The cover is equally important to sales. My cover was done by a friend, and while we worked on it with great intentions, it didn't show the readers what the book was about, it didn't catch your attention, and it didn't speak to the genre at all. We'll talk covers in chapter 5.

The title reflects the genre and hooks the reader, not to mention it's also a keyword that can help you be found in searches. My title was somewhat better, because once you know what the book is about (a girl named Evalene, who's given a number), then it's fairly memorable. But the girl's name is unusual and that in itself can make it hard to remember. We'll talk more about titles in chapter 6.

The back blurb, which is also sometimes called the "synopsis" or "back cover copy" among other things, is that short description of the book on the back cover that tells the reader what the story is all about. For the sake of this book, we're going to refer to this back cover description as the back blurb from now on. The back blurb for *Evalene's Number* was probably what I did best when I launched my debut, but on the Amazon book sales page I ruined all that hard work by putting a less exciting tagline first, before the blurb, using up that valuable real estate with other information and detracting from the *hook* I'd created in the blurb. More on blurbs in chapter 7.

A tagline or promotional line (aka a quote or short phrase that gets readers excited about the story) isn't necessary, but if you have the opportunity to include one and the space on your cover, then it'd be crazy not to! I wish I had a tagline on my debute. I didn't know at the time that this was a thing, but I've since heard that taglines are strongly recommended to authors as they are a key selling point. More on taglines in chapter 8.

Interior formatting has a less visible purpose than the others I've mentioned so far. But imagine you've hooked a reader with an amazing cover, title, and blurb, and then they flip to the interior and it's so dense that it's unreadable. They can't get past the first few paragraphs. You BET that will deter sales as well as reviews and future reader purchases. More on formatting in chapter 9.

Editors play a bigger role than most readers will ever know. If you've written anything, you know that certain typos and grammatical errors can become almost invisible to you, while someone else can pick up your writing and catch them at a glance. An editor does so much more than fix typos, however. They work with you to find plot holes and issues with the story as a whole, as well as make sure it's grammatically correct, clear, consistent, interesting, and not repetitive. An editor is crucial to creating a quality book! More on editors in chapter 10.

Keywords involves the searchability of your book, which if you remember from the introduction is one of the major ways sales happen. The more searchable your book is on Amazon, the more sales you will have—pretty straightforward right? More on keywords in chapter 11.

Categories refers to your book's place on the virtual shelf. Amazon and other online retailers like Barnes & Noble or Kobo or Book Depository all place books into categories, which include the genre, but go much deeper into sub-categories. For example, fantasy has sub-categories like "dark fantasy" or "myths and legends" or "sword & sorcery" and so on... More on categories in chapter 12.

And finally, YOU, the author. You have AMAZING marketing power in just being yourself, being present online, and being excited about your book. In chapter 13, I want to spend a ton of time on the seven marketing mindsets that you can develop that will help you be more comfortable talking about your book and selling it naturally.

These mindsets will be applicable to any of the marketing tools you choose, whether on social media, in newsletters, in blogs, in person at conferences or speaking events, or wherever else you decide to show up. Learning to talk about your book and sell it to the best of your ability is extremely valuable to selling more books.

In chapter 14, we'll talk about how to choose the right tools for *you* and *your* book, as well as why you should become an expert in those targeted areas instead of spreading yourself too thin and not accomplishing anything.

Alright! That's the big picture summary of everything we're going to discuss in this book—now let's dive in!

CHAPTER 4:
THE GENRE

"The best marketing doesn't feel like marketing."
—Tom Fishburne

EVERYTHING ELSE WE'LL talk about in this book could easily be figured out *after* you write it. But that's not the case with genre.

Genre matters more than most authors realize.

It matters far more than Mandi or I ever comprehended when we first started out. That's not to say you can't write the genre of your heart. But in this book, we're talking about how your book sells itself, so that means we have to have an honest talk about this subject.

And the truth is:

Some genres sell better than others.

And I mean a *lot* better.

Like, night and day difference.

When I wrote *Evalene's Number*, I wasn't considering the genre at all and only when it came time to find its place on the virtual bookshelf, did I actually stop and ask myself what it truly was.

Technically it's a dystopian. It also has Christian elements. It could also fall under science fiction and even in minor ways under fantasy.

This is what's called a *genre mash-up.*

And it's *not* something you want to do!

From my personal experience, I can tell you that if a reader isn't looking for a book like yours, and there isn't even really a name for the exact genre you've written, then unfortunately you've written something no one is looking for.

Be very careful not to write something no one is looking for.

I know that sounds harsh. I don't mean to be harsh, but I do want to be honest.

I'm not saying it won't sell at all.

Because—and please hear me when I say this—I'm not saying that any particular genre is bad. Even genre mash-ups can be amazing. And you *do* still have the ability to explain your book to people, to get them excited about it, and to make sales that way.

What I *am* saying is that it may not sell AS WELL.

Because if strangers aren't looking for it on their own, then it's not going to be on their radar. You're basically doubling your work load if you chose a genre that's less popular or not known at all.

Because now you have to put it on their radar in the first place.

Let's bring reverse engineering into play here. That means thinking of your target reader and putting yourself in their shoes when it comes to genre.

Most readers have favorite genres. They know the types of books they like. When they go out to buy another book, they look for something that fits that preference.

If you're writing a mash up of romance and thrillers (just to pick two that feel strange together), then both target audiences are going to be thrown off. The romance readers want the gushy stuff, but they're getting chase scenes. The thriller readers are rolling their eyes at all these long, drawn-out, "but how do you feel?" conversations… you get my drift.

Basically, a mash up is potentially alienating a large portion of your target audience.

But what about lesser
known genres?

You may have a clear "virtual shelf" in the online bookstore where your target readers can find you, but you may find that the pool of target readers is vastly smaller than in other genres.

Again, like I said above, this does not make the genre bad at all. It just means that you're naturally reaching fewer people.

I'm going to say something that I
won't say about any of the other
subjects in this book...

With the cover, title, back blurb, tagline, formatting, editing, keywords, categories, and your marketing mindset as the author, there are certain things that I really do think you should invest in and pursue. It's worth sacrificing your idea of a unique, twenty word title for sales. It's worth giving up your keywords that you like, for keywords that will actually ping your book when a reader searches. And it's definitely worth letting go of a conviction to never talk about your book for fear of judgement, and develop a marketing mindset as an author instead.

In all these other areas, I would say choose good marketing strategies over preference.

But when it comes to genre, again I'm going to say something that directly contradicts everything I've just told you. Something I won't say about *any* of the other ten tips in this book…

It's okay to choose a genre that won't sell as well, if that's what you want to write.

Why do I say that? Why do I say it's okay to ignore the genre rule?

Because you can't write what you don't love.

You just can't.

If you choose to write erotica because it sells so well, but you can't stand it, that's going to come across on the page. Readers can tell. They won't enjoy the story any more than you do. If you're writing contemporary, but you're wishing your story was in a fantasy world, your readers will be as bored as you. Or vice versa.

It's OKAY to make the choice to write what you love.

That said, you still need to go into this choice with your eyes wide open.

Because remember the truth I mentioned earlier:

Some genres sell better than others.

Plain and simple.

Before you settle on a genre, you need to be really honest with yourself and take a close look at the level of popularity. If you choose a smaller category with lower sales, you need to know that your sales numbers may be lower going into it.

What if I want to write what I love AND have it sell? Isn't there a happy medium?

I'm glad you asked, yes there is! There are a couple things you can do when it comes to genre and making sure that you're choosing a genre that both sells well and that you will enjoy.

The first option is to look at what you enjoy writing and see if you have multiple genres you're interested in.

What if you enjoy this tiny category over here, but you equally enjoy a booming category over there? If you find this is the case, then I'd encourage you to pursue the more popular genre.

This doesn't necessarily mean you're closing yourself off to other genres in the future, but rather choosing a focus for now. As your author career grows and you gain traction, you may have enough support from fans to pursue a smaller, lesser known genre in the future without hurting sales at all.

Maybe you find that in your two favorite genres, one of them will reach a small group of 1,000 target readers and the other will reach 100,000. That's a made-up scenario, but you get the idea. Which one would you choose?

The second option I'd suggest is to narrow your focus. For example, say you're like me and you have an idea for a mash-up. I wrote a story with Christian elements in a Dystopian world. Two genres that don't really intersect at all.

This is actually a very common thing for writers to do, because we love to be creative, and what better way than to create a brand-new genre altogether, right?

I've known people who wanted to write a contemporary story but threw aliens into the mix. If this was you, I'd ask, which one is the focus? And if you said both, then it probably wouldn't do well, because the genre is unclear. But if you pick one—pursuing just the contemporary and removing the aliens, or focusing solely on the story of the aliens and taking out the contemporary emphasis—this will set the book up for success, because the genre just became so much clearer.

If you have options, why not choose one that sets you up for success?

At the time of writing this, I looked up some stats that I wanted to share with you. Keep in mind that these stats change constantly and it's important to do your own research, not to mention it's extremely easy to google "genres that sell well" or "top book genres" or something along those lines. But this will give you a fantastic picture of how different genres perform better or worse than others.

What I found was that a huge number of online sales (aka ebooks) fell into one of four big categories (at least on Amazon).

Currently these four largest categories are:

- Romance: 40% of sales
- Mysteries/Thrillers: 20% of sales
- Fantasy: 6.33% of sales
- Sci-Fi: 5% of sales.

You'll notice that this is about 71% of book sales. Specifically, ebooks. There are completely different stats for paperback, hardcover, audiobooks, etc.

I repeat, do your research!

And here's what is really interesting—certain genres also do better in self-publishing while others do better in traditional publishing.

In those same four categories above, if you look into them, you'll find that sometimes self-published books completely dominate a category, while in others, traditional publishing is clearly the way to go.

Breakdown of Romance Sales

Self-published: 49%

Small/medium publishers: 11%

Amazon publishers (like KDP): 9%

Big 5/Harlequin: 30%

Breakdown of Mystery/Thriller/Suspense Sales:

Self-published: 11%

Small/medium publishers: 5%

Amazon publishers: 16%

Big 5 publishers: 68%

Breakdown of Science Fiction Sales:

Self-published: 56%

Small/medium publishers: 9%

Amazon publishers: 5%

Big 5 (plus Baen): 30%

Breakdown of Fantasy Sales:

Self-published: 49%

Small/medium publishers: 7%

Amazon publishers: 7%

Big 5: 37%

These are just the four big categories, for ebooks specifically, but there are SO many more!

Again, do your research.

And then go with what you love. Just make sure to pursue the genre with eyes wide open, knowing if it'll be an easy sell or a more difficult sell.

TIPS FROM MANDI:

It can be so hard to choose the genre of your own book. Often times, you're too close to the project to effectively decide how to categorize it. You'll notice when you explain your book to people that you describe it as, "a touch of romance with a hint of sci-fi and a little mystery that keeps you on the edge of your seat like a thriller."

As the author, you feel like your book contains every genre. How do you put it all into one category?

Sometimes the easiest way to figure this out is by asking someone else. Your beta readers and critique partners are great resources to ask their opinion on the genre. After they read the manuscript, ask them what genre they think the book is or what books they think are similar to it. An outsider's perspective can sometimes be the best perspective and this is what I do to discover the genre of some of my harder to place novels.

CHAPTER 5:
THE COVER

"Don't judge a book by its cover."
—Someone stupid

WHOEVER SAID THAT people don't judge a book by its cover lied to you (and to me). That's exactly what the cover is for!

Most readers make a snap judgment when they look at a book cover.

Is this the genre they like to read? Does it catch their attention? Is it beautiful and memorable?

There are always outliers, of course, but your typical reader will look at the cover before anything else and if they don't like it, they won't bother to look any further.

Your blurb could be fantastic. But it's on the back. Your title could be amazing. But if it's buried in graphics or the cover is overwhelming or the eye just slips past it, the reader will never know. Your interior formatting could be genius and revolutionary, but they're never going to open it to find out.

So the cover is the ultimate, number one factor in book sales and the first thing we need to get right.

I'm speaking from personal experience when it comes to cover mistakes.

I made some mistakes in the beginning, which I mentioned in the beginning of this book. When my friend and I designed the cover, it wasn't BAD. But there was no way to know what genre it was when you looked at it (VERY BAD), it didn't have anything particularly catchy in the imagery (NOT GOOD), and while it had some pretty colors, it wasn't remotely memorable (ALSO VERY BAD).

And like I mentioned previously, when I hired a cover designer for the sequel, *Pearl's Number*, I immediately saw the difference. As she designed mock ups for the second book, it made me question my first cover. Eventually, as you know, I hired my cover designer to rebrand the entire series and my only regret is not hiring them from the start.

#1 COVER ADVICE:
HIRE A PROFESSIONAL!

Unless you have a background in graphic design, specifically in designing book covers, you *really, really, really* should hire a cover designer.

Now, I did technically hire a friend with a graphic design background, but she'd never done a book cover before. So together we guessed our way through the process.

Can I tell you an embarrassing story? Almost 99% of my sales from the first book came from family and friends. People who knew me and trusted me enough to get past that confusing cover situation. Fast forward to when I released *Evalene's Number* again as "second edition" with the gorgeous new cover that speaks to the genre and is extremely eye-catching (I'd encourage you to go scope out the difference between the two covers online, just to see what I'm talking about!)... Wow. I'd say the majority of my sales now are to total strangers.

And can I just be super honest? I'm kicking myself for making this mistake, because I can only imagine what might have happened had I started with the second cover instead.

Family and friends would've still been on board, as well as strangers, and the sales would no doubt have doubled if not tripled during the release, which would've led to Amazon promoting my book more, which would've led to more sales, which would've led to more automatic promotion. Amazon rewards books that sell well with more exposure. We'll talk more about that in future books.

But I seriously can't imagine the enormity of this mistake and how much it may have affected my first book. And I want to help *you* avoid that mistake! My heart's desire in writing this book for you is to prevent you from having to learn everything the hard way, like I did.

#2 COVER ADVICE: THE MORE YOUR BOOK FITS THE GENRE, THE BETTER

The main problem authors have is that we love our book baby so much, and we want our cover to be "different." To "stand out." Which is a totally reasonable and understandable desire. But it took me so long to learn this second truth: **readers don't want a book that stands out.**

Maybe a better way to phrase it might be **readers don't want a book that doesn't look like the genre they love.** Standing out isn't bad, as long as it's standing out WITHIN the genre, and not in a whole different genre of its own.

Because when readers see a book that is clearly the genre they love, they're far more likely to grab it and start reading! And that's what you want!

This was so difficult for me to grasp, but once I did, as you know from above I immediately re-branded my debut novel, *Evalene's Number* with a new cover.

Suddenly I had a whole new group of readers interested in the book…

Because the cover speaks for itself.

It says, "Hi, this book is a dystopian science fiction with a story about a young man and woman in a world that is falling apart." How did it say all of that (and more) without words? You'll have to check it out on Amazon to see.

#3 COVER ADVICE: IT'S NOT TOO LATE

Maybe you've already published your novel like Mandi and I both had. That doesn't mean it's too late!

Obviously once your book has been published, changing the cover becomes a more serious undertaking.

It involves creating a second edition of the book, with a new ISBN number, and being extremely careful to let your readers know that it's the same book (unless you've drastically rewritten it as well), so that no one is upset if they purchase it a second time thinking it's a new story.

But it's completely possible and acceptable to make this choice. In fact, I'd like to challenge you to look into the traditional publishing world and discover just how many novels have been re-branded and re-released with new covers just to attract a more targeted reader-base.

If an experienced publishing company can sometimes get it wrong, then so can you and I.

There's nothing wrong with taking an honest look at your cover and admitting that maybe it could be better.

Our challenge to you in this chapter is to carefully consider your current cover if you're already published—or to make note of these questions if you're not yet published for when you do begin your cover:

1) Does it reflect your story and make a promise to the reader that it will fulfill?
2) Does it reflect your genre to the best of it's ability?
3) Does it line up with reader expectations for your genre?

What do I mean when I say making a promise to the reader? My favorite example I've ever heard was of an author who wrote a romance novel, but put a sword on the cover. The promise is that there will be action and adventure, and definitely some sword play. When readers picked it up, this was what they expected. Not a romance. It's not that the book itself was bad, but the cover was misleading. And because it attracted the wrong audience and didn't keep the cover's "promise," it received a lot of bad reviews.

If you have romance, make sure the cover promises romance. If you have fantasy elements, make sure the cover hints at these elements. If you have a lot of action, don't have a peaceful babbling brook on the cover. You get the idea.

What does your current cover promise? Does it come through? Is there more that you could promise that it doesn't hint at?

All of the above applies to reflecting your genre and meeting reader expectations for the genre as well. The author who put a sword on the cover of the romance book probably thought they would stand out as exciting and unique. But the genre expectations are there for a reason: because they work.

Your cover can stand out while still reflecting genre expectations. This is not the time or place to be unique. This is the time to essentially follow the crowd, because the crowd is going where the money is at. Make sense?

Again, you can still include gorgeous, unique aspects of your cover that make it stand out, while simultaneously fitting in. We're *not* suggesting to make a bland cover, by any means. Just use the knowledge of what *works* in your genre to your benefit!

If you're not yet published, you have the opportunity to set yourself up for a much higher level of success, by taking your cover seriously now. Get a cover designer who knows their stuff. It's worth it.

If you've already published, take the time to reconsider your cover carefully. Use the above questions to seriously evaluate your book. Is the answer to those questions yes? Or could you consider rebranding?

If you're interested in rebranding, check out our resources chapter at the end of the book, where we list some of our favorite links and resources.

TIPS FROM MANDI:

So what does a professional cover designer look like? Everyone has a friend who knows their way around photoshop, but there's a difference between being able to make yourself look skinny in a photo and knowing the basic elements of graphic design. I spent years learning different editing softwares before I felt comfortable calling myself a graphic designer.

A professional book cover has all these elements:

- *It looks great in black and white*
- *Images are balanced and seamless*
- *The text is readable*

Professionals also add an extra flare to their designs. A great example of this is how they use text. An amateur will just place the text on the cover. A professional will bring the text to life by giving it texture or an extra element that makes it stand out and gives even more tone to the book cover.

To see what I mean, try looking at the fiction books on your shelves and see what elements are included in the text. Usually fantasy covers are the best examples of this.

When looking for a cover designer, ask other authors who they used or just start searching Google. Cover designers can vary in price, and most times you get what you pay for. Before you pay your designer, make sure you do your research on them. Look at other covers they've made and look at their stock of pre-made covers to see their style.

A good cover designer will ask you many, many questions about your book so they can bring your book to life. All custom cover clients I work with have to fill out a form about their book that tells me everything I need to know, from elements of the book, to what important characters look like.

Always keep in mind that cover designers are artists, not mind readers. Communication with your designer is key to your dream book cover. Give them an idea of what you're looking for, but be open-minded. A cover designer is trained in graphic design and they know what works best in terms of design and the book's genre.

If you have any questions about the cover design process, feel free to reach out at:

mandi@stoneridgebooks.com

CHAPTER 6:
THE TITLE

*"Choosing your book title should be a combination
between marketability and sales copy."*
—Kindlepreneur

YOUR BOOK'S TITLE goes along with the cover in
a lot of ways—it's part of the design and if it's a turn
off that will be just as big of an issue as if the cover
is a turn off. But the title also matters because of
keywords, *length,* and *memorability*.

First, keywords.

Keywords are something we'll talk about in much greater detail in chapter 11, but they are essentially one of the search terms people can use online to find your book. These are more important with non-fiction than with fiction, but they play a role no matter what.

Your title is one of your keywords. When people search for a good book to read, what if you could find a way to make yours one of the first books they find?

For example, let's use this book you're reading now. When Mandi and I created this series, we thought back to when we'd first begun to research book sales. What was one of the exact search words we'd typed in? "Marketing for Authors."

We realized immediately that we weren't the only ones who had used that phrase, so when we began titling our series, we knew that "marketing for authors" needed to be part of our title.

Also, as we titled this book and future books, we made an effort to include the keyword "book/books" and "sell/sale/sales" as well as other keywords that relate to the more specific topics such as "social media" or "author platform."

How does this apply to fiction?

Not many people talk about this, because obviously keywords are more difficult with a creative story title.

When it comes to keywords in a fiction title, it may be less about choosing keywords that people search frequently, and more about making sure it doesn't include keywords that *are* searched frequently that would *detract* from your book.

For example, with "numbers" in the title, *Evalene's Number* and *Pearl's Number* often come up in searches alongside math books. How funny! But not necessarily what you'd want…

Or another great example would be if your title is extremely similar to others in your genre. It's a highly searchable keyword, but now your novel is competing with other books and a reader might choose to purchase one of those other books instead.

So, when it comes to fiction, I like to suggest carefully researching your title ideas in a Google search and an Amazon search. Maybe even a Goodreads search, which can show you books that aren't even being sold yet. What comes up? How would your book interact with those other titles on the same page? Would it do well?

Keep in mind that books are constantly changing and new books are being published every day, so you can't always guarantee that the Amazon or Google page will look the way it looks now during your research.

In my opinion, the best keywords for fiction titles are ones that still have *searchability* but with *lower competition.*

Finally, it's also wise to keep in mind that when it comes to titling fiction, other factors come into play quite a bit as well, and you still have other keywords outside of the title that will help readers find your book. (We'll talk more about this in chapter 11).

Ask yourself these questions:

1) Does this title have a lot of competition? Is there already a book out there with this title or a similar title? Book titles aren't copyrighted, but if it's a famous book or if it will appear in the same searches as your book, then having a similar title can confuse your readers.

Remember: confusion prevents sales.

2) Does this title have good searchability?
3) Would this title perform well on a page next to other books in this genre?

Consider genre.

The genre will heavily influence how your book is titled. The most obvious example is non-fiction versus fiction.

With nonfiction, you'll often see titles that have a catchy hook with additional extra title that is much longer than anything you'd ever find in fiction. It could be eight, ten, or twelve words long, and that would be seen as completely normal.

On the other hand, with fiction, you'll notice shorter, punchy titles. One, two, or three words are the most common. Sometimes four. More than that in a fiction title tends to be the exception to the rule. (Not counting the "tagline" or the "series title" in this number, although these come into play as well, and we'll talk more about both.)

You can break this down even more by noticing commonalities in a specific genre. For example, if you take a look at the titles in fantasy, I bet you'll notice some frequently used words. Some cheesy but true examples are: crown, sword, queen/king, castle, world, etc.

Or if you're writing romance, you might notice that those titles often have synonyms for love and romance, or synonyms for destiny, and there's a definite bent to using sexy, smooth, sultry words in the title.

Just like with the cover, it can be extremely wise to use a reader's expectations for a title in your genre to your advantage.

Ask yourself these questions:

1) Does this title promise something that the book delivers?
2) Does this title fit reader's expectations for this genre?
3) Would this title perform well on a page next to other books in this genre?

Length and Memorability

These last two, length and memorability, apply to books in ALL genres and they really go hand and hand, so let's talk about them together.

What's easier to remember: "Epic Novel" or "This Ambitious Designation of Imperturbable Inscriptions and Prose."

You can easily see the two issues with this second title. Not only is the length a huge issue (both of the title as a whole, as well as with the individual words), but it's obviously not a title you can easily spout from memory either.

Length

Length matters because a shorter title is easier to remember. But it also matters because of the "mouthful" factor.

How many times have you seen a novel reduced to an acronym? My favorite example, and the one that comes to my mind every time I talk about this, is *ACOTAR* (*A Court of Thorns And Roses*) by Sarah J. Maas. Can I just say that I still couldn't remember what the acronym stood for without looking it up? And don't even ask me to tell you what the other books are called.

Sarah J. Maas is a fabulously famous author who can get away with this. You and I, the average authors, cannot. I'm being dramatic here, because of course, you can do what you want. But if you're here for advice on how to sell more books and how to make your book sell itself (and I assume that you are), then I'd recommend against it.

The sweet spot for fiction titles is commonly known to be one to three words at the most. But I would argue that you could even be more specific, and say one to three *syllables* at the most.

YES, this is DIFFICULT. Us writers are verbose and we love using all the good words. Being forced to leave words out is torture. I can tell you right now that as I title my next series, I am *struggling* with keeping it short! But if you keep the "mouthful" factor in mind as you title your book, not only will your readers thank you, but it will lead to memorability…

Memorability

The memorability factor cannot be emphasized enough. I know we left it for last, but when it comes to your book title, it's my personal opinion that this is the most important thing to consider out of everything we've mentioned.

Imagine your reader needs to hear your book title five, six, or seven times to remember it. Now imagine a title that your reader hears once—just once—and it sticks with them. Which one will sell more books? Especially if they hear the title verbally and have no way to reference it again—if it's not memorable, they'll have no way to find it later, no way to look it up when they can't remember it, which equals a sale lost. But if they hear it and it sticks, then when they go to buy a book, they'll type in that memorable title and press purchase, and your title has just helped you sell another book.

Memorability also plays a key role in "word of mouth" sales, which if you remember from chapter 1 is ultimately one of three things that lead to book sales.

When a reader goes to recommend books to other readers, they're going to recommend what's memorable. I can picture actual scenarios where I've been talking books with a friend and drawn a blank as I told them, "You have to read this book! It's called... I'll have to look it up, I can't remember..." And then we move on, and that's another missed opportunity.

So when it comes to the three ultimate ways we sell books (word of mouth, searches, and reviews), you can see how your book title plays a vital role in both word of mouth and searches.

Does it have a hook?

This is a bonus question. After we've determined that our title has great keywords, a good length, and is memorable, one other question you can ask is, "does this title hook a reader's attention?"

I first learned the idea of a "hook" when it came to songwriting. It's the unforgettable element. It's like when you catch a fish with a hook, once it sinks in, they can't help but be reeled in. (Gross metaphor, I'm sorry, but that's where it comes from!)

A hook is a catchy, easy-to-remember title that reels a reader in.

Out of all the things we've just discussed, this is probably the hardest to define, because it's 100% based on gut instincts and creativity and opinion.

When it comes to creating a hook for your book title, this is what I tell myself and what I'd tell you:

1) The other factors are more important (keywords/length/memorability)

2) Don't settle—take your time pondering all of your options, because like anything creative, you can't rush or force this one

3) Research titles already published in your genre to find out what hooks YOU

4) Remember that it's still opinion based—what hooks you might not hook another reader, and vice versa, so don't stress over this quality too much.

Like any rule, these can be broken.

But if you do, you'd better have a good reason! Because there is great logic behind a short, memorable, catchy title.

If you knew that titling your book a genre specific, two-word title would sell ten times as many books as a creative, poetic, longer, "deep" title that you personally resonated with, which would you choose?

When you boil it down, a title is a business decision.

You don't have to completely sacrifice your creativity—just like with covers, I'd actually say it takes *more* creativity to find a title that is punchy, memorable, fits genre expectations, and yet still stands out.

I believe in you. You can do this. It'll take time, but it'll be worth it. Now go think up that bestselling title!

TIPS FROM MANDI:

When my readers see my book on a shelf, I want them to know two things right away: genre and the atmosphere of the story. We talk about how you can create this with the cover, but you can also create this with the title of your book. A title can be like poetry. It's short, but it can still evoke emotion.

For example, my debut novel Essence *wasn't always titled* Essence. *I had originally titled it* Phantom Lagoon, *which was the name of a place in the story. The title seemed cool at first, but it didn't give the right mood. Phantom Lagoon made the story feel dark, maybe a little scary. The story wasn't scary, so I changed the title to* Essence. *Now just basing the story off the title, you can get the sense that the story is mystical, maybe a touch of darkness, but overall, mysterious.*

When you're picking your title, think: how do I want my readers to feel?

CHAPTER 7:
THE BACK BLURB

*"We've all heard someone say, 'Man, it was so great...
I just can't describe it!' If you want to be a successful
writer, you must be able to describe it, and in a way that
will cause your reader to prickle with recognition."*
—Stephen King

IF THE COVER and title catch a reader's eye, what
do they do next? They turn the book over to read the
back! (Or on Amazon and other online stores, they
click the little description box.)

So it stands to reason that the blurb is also vital to book sales.

Whether you're about to publish or have already published, it's worth reviewing your blurb to see if it's selling your story to the best of its ability.

Some good questions to ask yourself when you're reviewing your blurb:

1) *Does it introduce the protagonist right away?* People don't usually care about a book until they know who they're supposed to care about. Which leads to the second question…

2) *Why should they care?* What makes your main character worth reading about? What makes them relatable? What makes the reader resonate with them and therefore want to know more?

3) *Do you have a hook?* You remember that fish hook we talked about in the last chapter

that reels a reader in? Usually you can hook a reader with the initial conflict, sharing just enough of it to grab their attention and make them want to know more. If you tell them too much, and answer the questions you raised with the hook, then they won't have a reason to read on and find out more. And of course, that means you need to ask...

4) *Have I given away too much?* Because the moment they're hooked, that's when you leave them hanging and desperate to read more.

5) *Is there anything I can cut?* If there are places you could use one word instead of three, do it.

6) *How can I tighten this up?* If you can find more fitting verbs, replace them. This is such a tiny, powerful couple of paragraphs that every single word counts. Challenge each word and ask, could it be better?

Give your blurb some tender love and care. And then test it out.

My favorite way to test a blurb is on strangers, because they will be much more likely to tell you their honest opinion when/if something isn't working.

You can try using different online communities, such as facebook beta reader groups or the beta reader forums on goodreads or something else altogether. Get creative. Put the time in to get multiple opinions.

Here's how you know when your blurb is ready: Strangers start saying, "I would read that book!"

Friends and family are often (hopefully) more encouraging of your work than strangers. So it's very possible that if you test your blurb on family and friends, they might give it the thumbs up before it's truly ready. Not that you can't ask them to help you, and they could still give amazing advice! But my test to find out if my blurb is finally, truly ready to sell the book for me, is to run it by complete and total strangers.

They're not invested in your success or your author journey. They don't know you at all. Of course, there will still be a range of opinions, and some people will be nicer than others. (Be prepared for a curmudgeon or two who might be harsher than you'd like!) But generally, you'll get a lot of great feedback, so thicken your skin and share that baby.

Ultimately, you will know you've written a good blurb when you post your latest revision and instead of the majority of people finding issues, you'll get a flood of excited readers asking where they could find this story.

You've done it! That's a fantastic blurb!

TIPS FROM MANDI:

After my debut novel, Essence, *was out for about a year, I realized something: when I was describing my novel to people in person, it wasn't the same blurb that was on the back of the book.*

When I first published the book, I was afraid to give away too much information. I didn't want to mention anything past the inciting incident. But guess what? The most interesting part of Essence *wasn't that she was losing the will and control of her body, it was that after she succumbed to that will, she became an Essence and her parents thought she was dead.*

For so long, I didn't want to reveal what this thing was that was possessing this girl, but I realized very quickly that wasn't the story. The story was what happened after, and that's what hooked people into the book. The book wasn't about a girl being possessed. It was about a girl who was trying to help her parents deal with her supposed death after she became an Essence.

After I changed the blurb for Essence, *I was able to explain the book to potential readers more easily and saw an increase in sales. I only wish I had written the blurb that way to begin with!*

CHAPTER 8:
TAGLINES/
PROMOTIONAL LINES

"A tagline is a catch phrase. It doesn't tell you anything specific about the story, but it does give you a feel for it..."

—Writers Helping Writers

A TAGLINE OR promotional line can mean so many things. Depending on which kind you go with, they could be written by you or by another author or by a reputable company, but the idea of these extra promotional lines is simple: grabbing your reader's attention.

Taglines and promotional lines aren't just a book-marketing tool either. They're a general marketing tool, because they're powerful! For example, a tagline that was created for Nike in 1988 but is still memorable to this day over twenty years later is, "Just Do It."

What is a tagline?

A tagline is like a catchphrase or a punchy one-liner typically written by you (or your publisher) to hook a reader in roughly 9-10 words or less.

Let's use an example of a fantastic one-liner on the cover of one of our favorite authors, Kim Chance. Her YA novel, *Keeper*, has a tagline at the top of the cover that says, "Magic always leaves a mark." It's a theme in the book, which makes it especially memorable after reading. It also hints at the story, by letting you know right up front that this book has magic and there are consequences for using this magic. Fantasy readers everywhere will appreciate this!

Another great tagline is from the extremely popular novel, *The Hunger Games,* which says, "Winning means fame and fortune. Losing means certain death. The hunger games have begun…"

You can see from these examples (and many more if you do your research on book covers online), that the tagline always hints at an *important* aspect in the book that will draw in *target* readers.

What is a promotional line?

A promotional line is just my broad umbrella term to cover everything else you could use to advertise your book, specifically on the cover.

Some examples of promotional lines are "praise for the book" from other authors or authorities in the publishing world and "achievements" such as "Amazon Best Selling Author."

Praise for the book:

One of my favorite examples of a promotional line is the **"praise for the book"** promo. These are always written by someone else, always a credible source, and usually by an author who's published a novel in the same genre as your book.

When I released the second book in The Number Series, I asked two close author friends who wrote in a similar genre if they would each write a short promotional line of praise for the book. If you're curious to see what they wrote, I'd definitely encourage you to check out the back of *Pearl's Number* or scroll down in the description on Amazon to see what they said!

If you're interested in going this route, you would want to make sure your praise is coming from a credible source, typically a published author. It's also usually recommended that they write in the same genre as you, so your audience will recognize their name.

Praise in general can be great, and if you have praise from beta readers that you're dying to use somewhere, you could definitely consider creating a page inside the book or below your description on Amazon of general praise, such as, "what early readers are saying" and that would be fantastic promotion.

But using a source that your readers will recognize for that main promotional line on the cover will give it a lot more "oomph." It's someone with authority in your reader's eyes saying to them, "This book is worth your time."

In traditional publishing, you'll even see many times that more than one author's praise for the book is included. You'll also notice that they can be placed in many different ways—I've seen these types of praise on the front cover (if they're short), the back cover, or even the inside flap of the book.

What should they write?

If you have a relationship with a credible source who's willing to write a promotional line or two for you, then some things they could include in their praise are:

- High excitement words like fast-paced, thrilling, adventure-filled, action-packed, exciting, etc.
- A call to action. An example of a call to action might be, "readers of such-and-such genre MUST buy this book!"

- A comparison of some kind. This is one of my favorites and can reference other books, genres, or authors. An example of this would be something like, "Fans of (this book title) and (that book title) will love (your book title)."

- Encourage them to read other praise for books and even send them some of your favorites, to give them a frame of reference.

If you're curious to see an amazing promotional line, just flip this book over to take a look at the back cover (or view the back cover on kindle) to see an example from our talented friend and fellow author, Jessi Elliott.

Achievements:

Another great type of promotional line is one that you should obviously only use if it's true: any notable writing achievements, usually specifically related to sales can be included on the cover.

For example, on the cover of *Twilight* by Stephenie Meyer, we see "The #1 New York Times

Bestseller." This is awesome for a reader to see because it provides credibility for the author.

Some other promotional lines like this could be "U.S.A. Today Bestselling Author" or "Amazon Bestselling Author"—again ONLY if these things are true! Lies will be found out!

These types of promotional lines give you authority as well, as long as they're accurate.

Like I mentioned in previous chapters, setting yourself up for success and the best book sales possible means imitating what works. And if you look at some of the bestselling books out there on Amazon or in Barnes & Noble, you'll quickly notice that taglines and promotional lines are very common.

Are taglines and promotional lines required?

No. You'll also notice there's a lot of fantastic bestselling books that *don't* have taglines. If you don't feel comfortable having one on your book or you just can't think of one, that's okay.

Including a tagline just for the sake of a tagline isn't the goal here. The goal is *memorability* and a *hook.*

Maybe even just one word is memorable? Or maybe your title needs to stand by itself to truly work its magic. Only you (and a test group) can determine that. (Notice how I subtly brought up getting multiple opinions?)

But maybe you have a memorable phrase inside the book that you stumble across while editing, whether in the prose or the dialogue—dialogue makes for some amazing one-liners by the way! Use that. Check out your back blurb and see if there's any line in the blurb that could also be pulled out to stand on its own on the front. It's okay to repeat something if it's catchy and memorable.

Unlike the cover, the title, and the blurb, the tagline will not make or break your book. But it can't hurt! You have all that valuable real-estate on the front cover and what if an extra couple words could sway your readers into buying your book? Seems worthwhile to me!

TIPS FROM MANDI:

Not sure if taglines are for you? If you look at my first three novels, you'll notice none of them have taglines on the front cover. Instead I put my taglines on the back cover and it's the first thing my readers see when they flip over the book.

Even if you don't have a tagline, at least try to come up with one sentence that will hook people into learning more about your book.

Here are some examples of my taglines:

Essence*: Essence. Something that exists spiritually, not physically.*

I am Mercy*: Imagine living in a world that looks at you as a curse.*

She's Not Here*: One life in exchange for thousands, maybe millions. Wouldn't it be worth it?*

Are you hooked into learning more about the books?

CHAPTER 9:
FORMATTING

"Amateur self-publishers are often tempted to 'dress up' their books with an abundance of fancy fonts. Resist this temptation! You want readers to notice your words, not the fonts they're dressed in."
—WritingWorld.Com

FORMATTING MAY NOT directly affect as many sales as your cover, title, and blurb, but there will definitely be people who choose to read the excerpt before purchasing the book. The level of professionalism and readability can directly affect their decision to buy your book and/or give it a good review.

The same thing applies to editing, which we'll talk about more in the next chapter. A typo or twenty, grammatical errors, or even bigger issues at the developmental level like plot holes can frustrate readers.

When the reviews start coming in, I guarantee they will reflect the quality of your work and ultimately have a huge effect on your book sales.

What is good formatting?

There are some rules when it comes to formatting as well as a good number of subjective opinions. Ultimately, good formatting is well done when it is pleasing to the eye and easy to read. It flows smoothly and isn't jarring to a reader.

In non-fiction like this book, it means breaking up your chapters into bite-size sections like this one here. It also means making sure paragraphs don't get too long and dense.

In fiction, good formatting could also include style choices like unique fonts and imagery.

Formatting also includes things like chapter headers with titles and/or numbers, making sure the chapter header starts halfway down the page, and indenting the first paragraph *except* when it's the first paragraph in a chapter, etc. There are quite a few rules when it comes to correctly formatting a novel, which is yet another reason why an editor is extremely important (more on editors in the next chapter).

Ultimately though, good formatting is about readability. If it's distracting a reader from the content, then it's not doing its job correctly. So a good question to ask yourself when it comes to the interior of your novel is:

What does your formatting look like?

Whether your book is already published or you haven't even gotten to this stage yet, I feel confident that most of us didn't come out of the womb knowing how to format a novel.

Your options when it comes to formatting are learning how to format from scratch, hiring a formatter, or there are also some options in-between those two extremes.

If you hire a formatter, you can often find them in conjunction with your cover designer. There are some great deals out there for formatting. If you're not a detailed person or learning difficult technical stuff irritates you, then this may be the right choice for you.

Shop around and see what you find. There are some absolutely gorgeous formats out there that are far more eye-catching than anything most of us could do. Maybe you'll find that it's worth the price for your book. Or maybe seeing the prices will convince you that you can learn how to do this step yourself.

Another option is to use software created specifically for formatting. One software that I know of is called "Vellum." This software is developed specifically for macbooks, but there is also a version for PC's.

Vellum is an intuitive program that can help you format your novel with a slight learning curve, and while it's a bit expensive, it's a one-time purchase that you can use on all your future books versus hiring a formatter for each book, thus saving money in the long run.

This is just brushing the surface. I've also heard of other programs, such as Adobe Indesign (a high level professional formatting option).

The last option is to learn how to format from scratch aka manually making formatting changes to the document yourself. The good news is that, at the time of writing this, there are templates available that give you a starting place and some tips for beginners, so even this option is not truly from scratch.

My favorite templates are found on a website called diybookformats.com by Derek Murphy. I highly recommend these templates and have used them to format all of my books to date.

In the resources section, I'll include a link to this template as well as to my YouTube tutorial where I teach how to format using this template in Microsoft Word. I'll also link Mandi's YouTube tutorial on formatting where she teaches a similar type of formatting starting from scratch.

Whatever you choose to do, know that formatting does influence whether or not readers enjoy your book, which then can lead to good or bad reviews. And reviews, of course, are a huge part of book sales.

But while formatting plays a role in how people perceive your book, the way a book is edited, which we'll talk about next, is even more important!

TIPS FROM MANDI:

Bethany and I both format our books ourselves because it's a huge cost savings. With that said, formatting can be a huge headache, especially if you aren't familiar with the tips and tricks of Microsoft Word.

If you plan on formatting your book yourself, give yourself a lot of extra time to do it, especially if it's your first time formatting a book, because there can be a steep learning curve.

If you need guidance, Bethany and I have left some resources and how-to videos (which you'll find at the back of this book) that will help walk you through formatting your book in Word.

CHAPTER 10:
EDITING

"The romantic myth of an author sitting alone in their room and emerging with a finished book is just that: a myth… working with [professionals] is absolutely crucial when writing a book."
—Reedsy

IT IS EXTREMELY rare to read a quality book that didn't have an editor in some capacity. In fact, I honestly don't know of any.

Having a professional review your work is vital to selling books for the same reason as formatting. If you have a book riddled with errors at any level, whether punctuation and grammar, or plot level problems, readers will leave bad reviews on your book that will be a clear sign to future readers not to buy your book.

Not only does this clearly the hurt sales of your current book, but it will also hurt your future book's sales as well, because readers *will* remember you.

I have a degree in English with a writing emphasis and attended college with the intention of being an editor at a publishing house. And I still need an editor! Not only do I make sure to have professionals review my work, but I also consistently ask friends and family to proofread as well. The more eyes on the story before publication, the better!

Why is this so important?

There's such a thing as "writer's blindness" which is a term for when you've gotten too close to your work and can no longer see glaring errors on the page.

Your eyes might skim over a spelling error twenty times, but your editor's eye is trained to spot them. However, even your editor is only human and can miss things as well, which is why I guarantee that everyone reading this can think of at least one book they've read in the past that had typos. Probably more than one. This is, again, the reason I aim to get as many eyes on my books as possible, including an editor.

Depending on what type of editor you hire, they are also trained to have different focuses, such as developmental issues (like plot holes and big picture problems), style issues (like repetition, awkward language, confusing language, etc), and technical issues (making sure things like grammar, punctuation, and spelling are in accordance with industry standards).

So the question you should be asking yourself here is:
DID YOU HIRE AN EDITOR?

Please, please hire an editor. Especially for your debut novel. I truly believe it's important to have a trained professional help you with every single book you write to truly create a quality book.

If you can't afford to hire someone who is an editor for a living, see if you can find someone with training and an eye for detail, such as a former English teacher or a college student studying to be an editor in the future. If you go this route, I recommend as many of these substitute-editors as possible, as they won't be at the same level as a professional and are bound to miss more or suggest incorrect edits.

It all boils down to this: the more eyes on your book before publication, the better.

Beta readers and critique partners are also invaluable to creating an excellent book. While I'm not going to go into detail on betas and CP's, the same things that I discussed above when it comes to an editor also apply here.

Beta readers, critique partners, and editors all catch different aspects of your book that need to be improved, helping you craft the most quality book possible.

Imagine your current story has ten plot holes and a hundred typos. Your beta readers and critique partner catch the first five holes and fifty typos. During rewrites, you add two new plot holes and twenty more typos. Your editor catches all the plot holes and the next fifty typos. Then your proofreader comes along, or a few friends and family, and they catch the last twenty typos. You take a deep breath of relief because now on release day your readers will never see those issues. You won't get dozens of angry reviews that the book didn't make sense because "this character died and then they were in the next chapter" or "the text was riddled with plot holes and I just couldn't finish."

Enough said.

This book isn't about writing and publishing, so as much as I could continue talking about editors, beta readers, and critique partners for hours, I'm not going to spend any more time on the how-to's for these steps.

I will leave it at this: make sure your book is fully-edited, both by yourself and by others, because this will affect sales as well as reviews (which indirectly affect sales as well).

TIPS FROM MANDI:

Like Bethany said, we could probably write an entire book series on writing and publishing, or just editing alone! But if there is one thing I can't iterate enough when it comes to editing, it's to get as many eyes on your book as possible before it's published.

Even a professional editor will miss some things. I've learned the hard way after I go through my copy editor's edits, that I need to give my book to my mom for her to read through (for the first time) and go through it with a fine-tooth comb.

She's not a grammar queen of any kind, but she's been known to spot even the most hideous typos that I cringe at when I realize no one had spotted it up until that point.

Give your book to a few people to read after it's been through edits and see if there are typos or other issues that may have been missed. A fresh pair of eyes is always a good idea.

CHAPTER 11:
KEYWORDS

"Keywords allow your book to be discovered by hungry shoppers [online] even while you sleep."
—Dave Chesson

WHEN I SEARCHED Amazon for how many books had come out in just the last 30 days, it had over 50,000 results. In just one month!

What that tells me is that unless you find a way to guide readers to your book, they aren't going to find it.

The point of keywords (and categories which we'll talk about in the next chapter) is to help readers searching for your specific type of book to find it. Note that I said specific type. Oddly enough, the more specific you can get, the better.

Have you ever heard the saying "big fish in a little pool, versus small fish in a big pool?" That's kind of the idea here. Maybe you have a great category or keyword that's super popular and loved, but that means it could have 100,000+ books under that category to compete with, or it could be searched 100,000+ times a day if it's a keyword. On the other hand, if you find a smaller keyword or category that reaches maybe only 1,000 people, your book may actually have a chance to stand out.

Before we delve into keywords...

I want to start by saying there are entire books dedicated to figuring out keywords (and categories). I'm *not* an expert by any means.

My focus in this chapter and the following chapter on categories isn't on giving you a breakdown of the exact keywords and categories to use for your book (because every single book is different and I'm here to tell you that you HAVE to do your research), but more to help you understand what keywords and categories *are* and *why* they're important.

What are keywords?

Keywords are words that define your content and help people searching those particular words to find you.

If you have the right keywords that people are searching for and that accurately describe your book, then people will find it!

If you have a book about a dog breed like Corgis for example (ahem… *The Confident Corgi*), then a keyword to use would be "corgi." Seems obvious, right?

Crazy dog ladies everywhere searching that term will be much more likely to find the book if it's listed as one of the "keywords" people are searching.

Keywords are part of SEO (Search Engine Optimization). Side note: I feel like this is the part of the book where I need to repeat that I'm not an expert, because I'm far from dialed-in here, my focus is writing books!

But that said, keywords play a huge role in your book sales as well as other areas of the internet, such as how people find your author website, for example. So it pays to be aware of keywords and learn how they affect your books.

While they play a big role all over the internet, I'm going to focus solely on how keywords will help with book sales.

Why are keywords important for book sales?

I'm glad you asked! Let's use a few metaphors for kicks to help you understand the role keywords play.

Imagine that a keyword is like a library reference number that you need to find a book in the library. If you're given the wrong reference number, you're not going to find it.

But if the library provides the correct reference number, then every time someone wants to read that book they are taken right to it.

Keywords are a CONNECTOR. And with all the info available on the internet right now, this is crucial.

Imagine now that you get to have multiple reference numbers. Sounds great, right? On Kindle Direct Publishing for example, you get seven keyword options, plus the title is technically also a keyword opportunity!

Sounds extremely valuable, and it is—if you're giving out an accurate reference number (aka keyword). But if you're using the wrong ones than you could have a hundred reference numbers/keywords and still fail to help readers find your book.

To use the corgi book as an example again, if I use the keyword "cat" for a book about a dog, then my library reference number is sending people to the wrong section and everyone who's over there browsing that section is looking for cat books so they're going to pass right over a dog book.

Same thing is true for your book. If you're accidentally misdirecting people by using the wrong keywords, then you're placing your "dog" book in front of "cat people." Make sense?

So how do you know what the right keywords are?

This is where it gets tricky. There's a LOT of science behind this, and I repeat for the bazillionth time that I'm not an expert by any means.

On top of which, the things that I've discovered work for my books are very unlikely to work for your books, because every single book is unique. I can't even apply what I've learned with my dystopian series to my fantasy series, because it's an entirely new animal.

You have to do your research.

I know, just what you wanted to hear. The way I see it, you have three options.

1) You can continue to put your "dog book" in front of "cat book" people and not sell much of anything.

2) You can teach yourself through trial and error. There's a lot to be said for taking the time to test different keywords until you start to see more traffic and purchases. **Keywords aren't set in stone. If they aren't working, you can change them!**

3) Your third option would be to go to experts. The good news is there are a lot of brilliant, talented people out there who are willing to teach you. There are tons of great articles, videos, tutorials, and even books specifically for authors to understand and learn to choose the right keywords for their books.

In the resources chapter, we'll include a few helpful links to get you started. Don't be afraid to try some keywords, take notes on what is and isn't working, and then change it up until you find something better.

Now let's move on from keywords to the other half of what helps readers find your book online: categories.

TIPS FROM MANDI:

Choose your keywords carefully. And by this I mean make sure the keyword, if on its own, speaks for itself and the book. For example, my third novel She's Not Here is a psychological thriller about a nurse that begins experimenting on a child in an attempt to find a cure to Alzheimer's. When I set up the book for pre-order, I added "Alzheimer's" as a keyword. After people began buying the book on Amazon, it quickly got high on the best-seller list...for Alzheimer's.

Why was this bad? Because every other book on that list was a non-fiction book about helping a loved one with Alzheimer's. I didn't want someone looking at the best-seller list buying my book thinking it was something it's not.

You need to choose keywords that fit in your genre. While choosing unfit keywords may help you rank on Amazon and maybe even sell more books, it will hurt you in the long run if someone buys the book thinking it's a different genre, therefore leaving you a bad review and affecting future sales of the book.

CHAPTER 12:
CATEGORIES

"If you can't explain it to a 6-year-old, you don't know it yourself."
—Albert Einstein

CATEGORIES ARE YOUR book's spot on the virtual bookshelf—similar to what we talked about earlier with genre, but far more specific.

If genre is like one long bookcase, then the categories are the individual shelves. And there are sub-categories within sub-categories within sub-categories.

Now I know that many (if not all) print on demand companies place books into categories, such as Ingramspark or Lulu or Barnes and Noble Press, and bookstores like Barnes and Noble do as well, so the number of categories may vary depending on the company.

But in this book I'm going to focus specifically on Amazon categories, which means I'm focusing on KDP (Kindle Direct Publishing).

KDP allows its authors to place their book into two categories.

Unlike keywords, these aren't whatever you're in the mood to type in, but are all a very specific, previously created virtual "shelf."

For example, with my young adult dystopian novels, I chose the big umbrella category of fiction, then focused on young adult fiction, followed by science fiction and fantasy, underneath which I chose science fiction specifically, and finally, underneath that I chose dystopian.

You'll need to spend time carefully researching the other books in your category to know if that category is right for your book.

The good news is, with Amazon you can actually see what categories other books are in! If you scroll down to the "Product Details" section of any book on Amazon, you'll see that there is an Amazon Best Sellers Rank and below that are the categories for that book.

TIPS FROM MANDI:

I've heard rumors you can have more keywords and categories on KDP (Kindle Direct Publishing). If you call KDP, you can ask them manually add the extra keywords and categories for you!

See the resources chapter for more information on how to do this!

But before you bother with that, start by getting your book into the initial categories correctly and getting the initial keywords right.

Do your research!

I repeat: research is key to succeed at keywords and categories. We'll include links to learning more about keywords and categories in the resource section at the end of this book, so you can spend time researching what will work best for your book.

Remember, if your readers can FIND your book on the virtual shelf, more readers will BUY your book.

CHAPTER 13:
MARKETING MINDSET

"Sometimes the questions are complicated and the answers are simple."

—Dr. Suess

RAISE YOUR HAND if you feel uncomfortable talking about your book. A lot of authors feel really awkward trying to advertise their work, or nervous to share their story for fear of judgment, or shy because they don't know if anyone will care.

If that's you, you're not alone. But let me ask you this, how can your readers support you and buy your book and read your amazing story… if they don't know it exists?

Your discomfort and fears are so normal, but you don't have to feel this way.

And if you want to sell books, let's be honest, we *can't* be this way! We *have* to talk about our book!

And let's get even more real. You can honestly love marketing and *still* not feel confident that you're doing it right.

Simply talking about your book is the biggest, easiest, most often over-looked, cheapest marketing tool.

You get new eyes on your social media, website, and newsletter constantly. Even people who've been around for awhile and heard your "spiel" could forget about your book and their plans to buy it. Which brings me to something called "The Rule of 7."

The Rule of 7:

In the marketing world, there's something known as the "rule of 7" which says that the average person needs to hear about a product seven times before they'll decide to purchase it.

Safe to say bringing up your book once in a blue moon isn't going to cut it, huh? Talking about something seven times can feel like a *lot* when it's coming from you, which is why I think it's really important that we talk about some different strategies for *how* you talk about it to make it feel more comfortable and come to you more easily.

These next strategies are my 7 Marketing Mindsets that will help you break out of your comfort zone!

MINDSET #1 - VIEW YOUR BOOK/WORK/SELF AS VALUABLE

View your book as valuable. Because it is! You love your story right? I'm assuming you think it's pretty amazing since you're choosing to spend a lot of time writing it. You put in all that work or are currently putting in the work to make it the best that it could possibly be.

So, telling people about something you truly believe in the way I know you believe in your work makes sense. Of course they want to read something amazing like your book!

On the flip side, you should never talk badly about your book and say it's not good, because that's actually marketing as well, just in the opposite way that you intend—basically negative publicity!

Your book is valuable. You know it's valuable, that's why you wrote it. So when you go to market it, remember to talk about what you're offering like the treasure that it is.

Avoid extremes…

Of course, because I'm all about balance, and I know that avoiding one extreme can cause people to go to the other extreme, I also want to mention that marketing should never be about pushing products down people's throats or constantly pressuring them to buy something.

I'm sure you've experienced this kind of marketing. Does it work on you? The best way to avoid coming across this way, is to come at marketing with the mindset of, "I've created something really valuable. I know it is worthwhile and people will love it. I want to help them discover something they will enjoy."

MINDSET #2 – BE GENUINE

If you approach marketing with this mindset, it will help you avoid being spammy. NEVER spam people. We all hate that. I'm sure you've all seen someone who says, "buy my book" in every photo or tweet or other format online.

What if instead, you share insight into your story, little tidbits that pique people's curiosity, little quotes from the book or stories about your author journey and how the book came to be. Something genuine, like, "I'm so in love with this cover and the way it turned out," or, "I'm over the moon excited about this review I just received, it was the sweetest, most encouraging, thoughtful blog."

Not only is this personal, fun, and gets others excited with you, but most importantly, it's 100% true.

Being genuine is the OPPOSITE of being spammy. If you need some help figuring out what this looks like I'd say post the way you would if you were talking directly to a friend.

Post like you value your readers time. Because honestly, which kind of post would you rather read?

MINDSET #3 – FIND A NEW WAY
TO SAY AN OLD THING

Try to keep things unique. It's totally okay to say things like, "link in bio" often if you want to make sure everything is easily accessible. Just remember:

Nobody enjoys hearing the song "buy my book" on repeat.

Honestly that's true about anything. Repetition can drive readers away. Mixing up your message to keep it fresh and unique can make the marketing process much more enjoyable for both your reader and YOU.

Say for example, that you're editing again tonight, for the five-billionth time in a row. You don't want to be repetitive and say this again.

Okay, share why you're struggling with a particular scene or how you had a breakthrough or talk about the chocolate you get to eat as a reward. Now it's unique.

Some ways you can come up with a new way to say an old thing, is to

- be more specific
- be more authentic and transparent

Like we talked about, being genuine is the opposite of spamming, so if you're being really open and honest, that's going to resonate with people.

MINDSET #4: THE RULE OF 7

We already talked about the rule of seven earlier, I know. But the reason I'm bringing it up here within these seven mindsets, is because it truly is a *mindset*. It's something you'll have to remind yourself of and cultivate this attitude toward marketing.

Approach your marketing with the understanding that it's OKAY to remind people you have a book!!!

I am so tempted to add more exclamations points to that, but I've already massively broken the rules of English grammar, forgive me...

I know *so many authors* who don't talk about their books. Why? A couple reasons. Often the root is embarrassment or fear or other emotions that generally attack us writers and make us afraid to share.

There's a lot of judgment when you're proud of something, isn't there?

But you *should* be proud of it! You worked so hard on this book, and it deserves you shouting about it from the rooftops. If you're struggling with fears, insecurities, or expectations of judgement, ask yourself this question:

Why did I write it?

I mean, that's a trick question. Because if you're like 99% of writers out there, then *you wrote it for someone to read it.*

Or maybe you're holding back because you've experienced an author who overshared.

You all know what I'm talking about. The people who sing the "buy my book" song on a daily basis. And by the way, to fall into this frame of reference, at least for me, you have to be pretty spammy. (I'm talking like an Instagram page full of ads of your book level spammy).

Don't forget: your typical audience needs to see a product SEVEN TIMES before they will consider buying it.

You can't just pop by once a year, or even once a month. You need to be consistent in reminding people about your book, especially if you have new people in your circle of influence who haven't heard about your book at all yet.

BUT like we just talked about, reminding people is 100% ineffective if it's shoving the same old thing down people's throats in a spammy way.

Which is why all these mindsets work together as one cohesive marketing strategy. When you go to remind people seven times, you're still being intentional about also reminding them in a NEW and GENUINE way as you tell them about the VALUE your book will bring to them.

MINDSET #5: YOU HAVE TO GIVE TO GET

If you're providing value to them—if you're giving them something, such as writing advice, fun tips, quirky thoughts, enjoyable photos, your time, whatever is specific to you and your author platform—you'll find that your audience will want to give you something valuable in return, such as purchasing your book, supporting you as an author, and even singing your praises from the rooftops.

People want to know you care about them before they care about you.

Determine what you can offer your readers that you truly believe is valuable. Spend time thinking on it. Maybe it's your time, maybe it's your resources, maybe it's encouragement, maybe it's something different with each person you interact with.

Think it over, do what's true to you and what you enjoy, but figure out a way that you can GIVE to people, because they will give back.

MINDSET #6: YOU'RE SELLING NOT ONLY YOUR BOOK, BUT ALSO YOUR BRAND

This mindset is especially helpful for those of you who do not have a book published yet. Whenever you market, you're selling both your book and your brand.

You may not have a book to sell yet, but you can begin marketing your brand TODAY.

I've talked about this before, but I wish I would've started marketing my brand much sooner! I can't even imagine where I would be today if I'd started marketing a year earlier.

When I say marketing your brand, what I mean is that whether you realize it or not, you're creating a public image of yourself as an author.

Is that image all about writing? Or is it all about what you read? Do you include other specific parts of your life as well? Such as your coffee obsession? Your cute fiancée? Your corgi puppy?

Or maybe you decide that part of your brand will include sharing deeper stuff, like your faith or politics (really would advise against that last one but you can do whatever works for you).

As you share specific parts of your life and work, you are creating a brand by telling people what they will get when they follow you.

I remember learning about branding and worrying over what I should "make" my brand... only to open Instagram to find not just one, not just two, but three messages from people about corgis— I had already begun to develop my brand without even realizing it! Your brand is whatever you choose to repeatedly share out of your passions.

This leads to asking yourself the question, how vulnerable and exposed do you want to be? What type of content do you want to focus on?

The more focused your "brand" aka content you prefer to share is, the more you can be certain the audience you attract will stay with you.

Your author brand should be more professional, at least to a certain extent, because that tells readers that you are taking it seriously, and allows them to trust that you are also taking your book seriously.

And goodness, I hope it goes without saying, but your author brand should include your writing! If you're creating these author platforms to ultimately sell books, then you'd better believe your brand needs to include your books. I think we all know this, but it's a good reminder if you're dealing with those insecurities and fears and judgments we mentioned earlier, to remember that this isn't bragging or oversharing, this is part of your brand.

It's totally okay to experiment with your brand, especially as you start out.

The only way to truly figure out what suits you best is through trial and error. Too many writers wait until they're perfect. I have some unfortunate news: Nobody is perfect. If you're waiting for that, then it's never going to happen.

Don't wait to start.

Which leads to my last mindset, and possibly the most important:

MINDSET #7: DON'T BE AFRAID TO FAIL

I wasn't sure if I should call this mindset "don't be afraid to try things" or "don't be afraid to fail." Both are true.

You're going to try marketing tactics that don't work. Expect it, accept it, and move on to the next thing.

Keep trying!

When you find something that works, spend time getting really good at it. But again, not everything will work, and there's nothing wrong with that.

Don't you dare feel like a failure and give up. Failing is totally normal and some of the most successful people have failed more than you and I ever will. The difference between a successful person and an unsuccessful person is simply that one of them won't give up.

There are about a billion other things you could try, we've counted, so if you ever encounter a marketing tip or trick that works for some people but doesn't work for you, don't despair. You're completely normal. Let it go, and move on to the next thing.

Summary of this tip: DON'T GIVE UP.

I hope these tips will help you fall in love with marketing and feel more confident about it. I've boiled down all the marketing mindsets into this one sentence below, which you can feel free to share if you find it helpful:

*GOOD MARKETING MEANS REMINDING YOUR READERS **REGULARLY** ABOUT ALL THE **VALUABLE** THINGS YOU WANT TO **GIVE** THEM OUT OF YOUR **OWN EXPERIENCE,** INCLUDING YOUR **BOOK,** IN A **NEW** AND **GENUINE** WAY **WITHOUT FEAR OF FAILURE**.*

TIPS FROM MANDI:

Embrace that you're an author! Imagine for a moment you're at your annual doctor's visit and the nurse asks you what you do. Say you're an author! I don't care if you have a day job that pays the bills or if you've only sold a few copies of your books to family members.

If you published a book, be proud of it and tell the world about it. If you don't tell people you wrote a book, how are they supposed to know to read it?

CHAPTER 14:
FINDING YOUR FOCUS

*"You can do anything, but you can't do
everything"*
—David Allen

LIKE I MENTIONED IN the introduction, there are
billions of ways to market your book.

It can be absolutely paralyzing.

If you're like us and most authors, you're probably trying to do it all. You're a smart, talented human, so you do your research. And then the online people or your friends or whoever, say to you, "Listen, you have to do A, B, and C. Seriously, if you're not doing this, you're not going to succeed."

So you do A, B, and C. Then you listen to that podcast that describes why "D" is absolutely essential. So you add that to your list. And when that talented author friend does "E," you know you better do it too. Then you see an article on how every successful entrepreneur should be doing F, G, HIJKLMNOP...

You get the idea.

Pretty soon, you're juggling this entire alphabet of things that you've been told you MUST do to succeed, but instead of success, you're feeling burnt out, frustrated, and confused. And maybe even a little annoyed at your book. Like, I'm doing everything they tell me to, so maybe it's the book's fault. Or maybe it's my fault.

NO. It's not your fault.

I'm here to say something that's going to be hard to hear. But again, you're pretty smart and you read the quote at the beginning of the chapter, so you probably saw it coming...

The problem is you're stretching yourself too thin.

You're dipping your toe in a million different pools, but you're not actually soaking up enough information to make a difference.

I think everyone would agree that if you're going to compete in the Olympics you need to be an absolute master at your sport, right? You would put the time in to be the best. If someone tried to compete in every single Olympic sport, they'd be laughed out of the competition.

Because everyone knows to win at something, to be the best at it, it has to be your FOCUS.

You have to give it more time. More energy. The more you put in, the more likely you are to succeed.

Same principle goes for marketing.

Say you try to do all the things at once: Instagram, Facebook, Twitter, Snapchat, Tumblr, YouTube, your website, giveaways, newsletters, online trainings, blogs, vlogs, book releases, book signings, events, amazon ads, facebook ads, etc.

What's going to happen? (Besides absolute burnout.) You're going to find that you're only able to dedicate a small amount of time to each of these things, and most, if not all of them, will suffer for it.

What if you were willing to be more focused?

For example, if you choose a particular social media, then you would begin to research everything you can get your hands on about that social media. How do readers interact with authors on that platform? How do authors sell books there? Research the best times of day to post, and how often, and different styles, and how to be successful on *that specific platform.*

The truth is, almost any platform can be successful, if you use it right.

But often you'll see a lot of authors trying to do it all. To use social media as an example again, many authors try to have a strong social media presence on every platform. They'll post mediocre pictures to Instagram, because they don't quite get that Instagrammers are all about the beautiful photos. And political rants on Facebook. Because technically, that's all people use it for these days anyway. I get it. And they'll tweet about their lunch, not realizing the potential on twitter for pitching your manuscript to agents!

I get why we feel like we have to do it all, but there's NO POSSIBLE WAY to be an expert in anything if you're spread that thin.

I'm not an expert in everything. But that's intentional.

Or maybe a better way to say it would be, I'm not an expert in everything because that's IMPOSSIBLE. The only way you could truly master even half of the marketing options out there would be if you were working on them full time.

But then when would you write your book?!

The important thing to remember is that you want to be an expert in WRITING, not marketing. Marketing is the side gig, right? So, this chapter is about us coming to the realization that we can't do it all, and we don't even want to, because that would take away from writing.

As unpopular of an opinion as this might be, I don't think you should be an expert in everything either.

Which leads to what I *really* want to focus on in this chapter. You CAN become an expert in a limited number of things. But more importantly,

It's better to be an expert in a few things, than useless in all of them.

Learning and understanding a marketing tool takes TIME and ENERGY. (And sometimes money!)

All of those things are precious. We don't want you to lose your mind over trying to do it all. Speaking from personal experience, that's the worst!

Have I convinced you yet? I hope that you see where I'm coming from, because I'm very excited to talk to you about a solution.

The solution starts with this exercise:

I want you to take a piece of paper and list absolutely every marketing tool you can think of—paid, unpaid, social media or otherwise, short term, long term, what you see other author's doing, even what you haven't seen other author's do that you think is a good marketing tool. Feel free to research, google ideas, pinterest some stuff—really spend time creating a good, long list.

Don't skip ahead until you feel like you've exhausted all the ideas you can think of. (If you need to, you can sneak a peek below where I list out a good chunk of what's out there, and add those to your list as well.)

Some tools:

- Facebook
- Instagram
- Twitter
- Tumblr
- Snapchat
- Patreon
- YouTube

- Pinterest
- LinkedIn
- Google SEO
- Your website
- Your newsletter/email list
- Your opt-in
- Business cards
- Your blog or vlog
- Forums
- Advanced Reader Copies (ARCs)
- Street teams
- Blog tours/vlog tours
- Social influencers
- Amazon Ads
- Facebook Ads
- Goodreads giveaways
- Regular giveaways
- Goodreads forums
- Promotions
- Discounts/sales
- Bookish events
- Book signings
- Networking events

- Conferences
- Guest posting
- Newspapers and other media outlets
- Press kits
- And of course, the book itself.

Now comes the hard part. I want you to pick THREE of them.

The reason we pick three, is so that you can **become an expert in THOSE THREE THINGS**. Whatever they might be.

Your challenge for this chapter is to choose what you're going to focus on going forward. What you want to *master*. What you want to know inside and out. What you want people to come to you for advice on, and watch in awe as you sell and conquer.

Just three.

I know, I know. Not possible. How can I possibly limit myself when I might be missing out on something that's pure gold? There's a name for this feeling: FOMO. (Fear Of Missing Out.)

It's a legitimate feeling. But it's holding you back from truly delving into real learning. Because that list of tools that we just made together—that's too much for one person. That's honestly too much for even a small team of people.

It can be really difficult to narrow your focus down to three things, but the reason for this is:

1) it makes marketing manageable for a solo-author-preneur like you and I

2) it frees you up to not feel guilty

3) It allows you to become an expert

If you are only able to devote 10 minutes a day (or less!) to each marketing tool, the odds that you'll master any of those skills is pretty low. Aka impossible.

But if you're willing to narrow your focus to just THREE specific tools (and yes, this is temporary, you're not committing to this for life), then you will allow yourself the freedom and time and energy required to utilize those three things to their fullest potential.

How about a more specific example from my personal experience: you could be invested in every single social media (plus everything else on the list), posting sporadically, struggling to keep up, to keep your head above the surface with only a handful of followers to show for it... OR you could choose to focus on one platform (*ahem* in my case, Instagram, my favorite), and invest time in researching how to use the app well, taking classes, studying what others do, investing hours into the platform, posting on a consistent, daily basis, and developing your following from a hundred or so people to thousands.

"So how do I choose my top three?"

My suggestion is to focus on:

1) tools you're passionate about and

2) tools where you see a lot of potential for your book.

For example, if you adore using technology, you might have a blast setting up your website or figuring out Google SEO. Or if you love working with people, your best focus might be things like street teams and garnering reviews.

If you're not passionate about your marketing tools, they become a hundred times more difficult.

You will likely approach marketing with frustration instead of excitement, if you don't love what you're doing. And readers will be able to tell. Despite what you hear sometimes, marketing can be *fun*. So choose what you enjoy.

The same thing applies to choosing a tool that has potential for *your* book. If you choose a tool that isn't a good fit it will make your job so much harder than if you choose one that fits perfectly. For example, if your book has an adult audience then Facebook is perfect because they mainly have an adult audience. On the other hand, Instagram is better for young adult novels, because it has a younger audience. If you were selling a cook book, you'd want to focus on Pinterest, where people often go to search recipes.

You get the idea. Take your time to figure out which tools will be best for *you*.

Remember FOMO (Fear Of Missing Out) is real and most authors feel it, but you don't have to *act* on it.

Someone might say "you have to do A, B, and C to succeed" when the truth is that "D, E, and F" are what will benefit you far more. Only you can know, so do your research and decide based on *your* needs, not anyone else's.

The good news is that your top three choices only need to be your focus for three to six months.

Every three to six months, depending on if/when you feel you've become an expert in your top three, you can re-evaluate your list and pick a new top three.

When you get to that point, you can ask yourself these questions:

- *Have I become an expert?*

Have you researched this tool and learned how to use it to the best of your ability?

- *Am I seeing results?*

Are you selling more books? And if not, is it because you haven't mastered it yet or is it because it's just not the best tool for you?

And if the answer is yes, you can then ask:

- *Can I put this on autopilot?*

Have you mastered it to the point that it comes easily to you now?

- *Should I continue using this tool?*

Is it going to be valuable for book sales and worth continuing, or is it taking up too much of your valuable time and resources? Are the results you're seeing worth your time and money?

As you become an expert using your top three tools, you can then add more to your tool-belt.

If, after a few months of learning and developing skills in three specific marketing tools, you ask yourself the above questions and find that either:

1) A skill has become almost automatic for you, or...

2) You can tell you're not seeing results and know you want to discontinue using this tool

Then either way, good news!

That's when it's time to ADD new tools to your tool-belt!

Whether you're removing a marketing tool altogether, or you just find that you have enough free time to add a new one, either way, you can update your top three as time goes on, becoming an expert in more and more marketing tools.

But you have to start somewhere.

Which leads to our second exercise:

It's time to pick your top three. You might have already, if I've been persuasive enough!

In this exercise, we want you to write your top three down here or in your notebook, as a commitment to yourself to focus on these three things and become an expert in them.

1) _____

2) _____

3) _____

Let go of ALL the other tools.

Let some of the stress and anxiety slip away and relax! You're not going to worry about any marketing strategies other than your top three in these next few months.

You're not going to think about them, not going to feel bad you're not using them, not going to worry about them for a second. Because you're becoming a master in your top three, and that's FAR more valuable to you in the long run.

For example:

When I narrowed my focus to three things, one of those things I chose to focus on, was reviews. Specifically, I focused on requesting reviews from bookstagrammers. Instead of just getting one or two random reviews, I was able to request and receive over ten times that many. People emailed and messaged me after my release asking, "How did you get so many great reviews?" The answer is I put my focus on this one specific method, put a lot of time into learning who to ask and how, to the exclusion of other marketing tactics. And that's what you need to do with your top three.

We're here to ask you tough questions, so get ready:

What's more important to you, selling books or trying every single marketing tool you can find?

Because you'd think that those two would overlap, but surprisingly they don't really mesh. I feel like I'm getting repetitive here, but it bears repeating. You can't do it all. Good marketing means marketing with skill and ease. And skill and ease come from familiarity, practice, and a lot of time devoted to the cause.

So buckle up, and decide where you're going to put your time. I'm not going to tell you what's best, because it's different for everyone. What do *you* enjoy the most? What do *you* see as an extremely successful tool? What comes easily to *you?*

Cool. Do that.

Should the Book Itself Be Included?

Yes! The reason I spent a whole chapter looking at all the marketing tools out there, and more importantly, encouraging you to FOCUS on just three of them, is because I firmly believe that *one of those three focuses should be your book itself.*

You may not be in this stage yet. Maybe you're writing your first draft or editing. Maybe putting together a cover, title, blurb, and so on is further on down the road for you. That's okay!

But at some point, every author has to make a decision about how much time and effort they're going to put into creating a quality book and helping it sell to its fullest potential.

I'm here to tell you that there's no better marketing tool to put your time and energy into than the book itself.

TIPS FROM MANDI:

If you're having a hard time finding the three tools that work for you, then give yourself a grace period to explore some of the tools out there. You don't have to have your three tools picked out right away.

Do some research or keep reading this book series to find what works for you!

Remember how Bethany said book sales come down to word of mouth, searches, and book reviews? With that in mind, answer these questions to find out what tools will help you grow:

- *What tool will help you network and utilize "word of mouth" as a marketing tool?*

- *What tool will help you and your book show up in search results?*

- *What tool will help you get book reviews?*

CHAPTER 15:
FINAL THOUGHTS

"An essential aspect of creativity is not being afraid to fail."
—*Edwin Land*

IF I'VE LEARNED ANYTHING from marketing, it's that we're always going to make mistakes. It's unavoidable. And that's OKAY.

Seriously. In my mind, I'm sitting across from you in the coffee shop right now, leaning forward to emphasize my point:

You're going to make mistakes.

Not only is it totally okay to make mistakes, it's AWESOME.

You might be thinking right now that I'm overly enthusiastic about this. And I should probably clarify that I'm definitely not saying mistakes are fun… But mistakes mean that you're trying—that you haven't given up. Remember the difference between successful and unsuccessful people? *Successful people don't give up.* So whenever I see someone making mistakes, to me that just means they're getting that much closer to success.

It's really easy to get caught up in the "what if's" and "if only's."

But don't.

Consider the shopping analogy:

Try to look at marketing more like a shopping trip where you're trying on clothes. This is a silly analogy, but bear with me:

Pretend you found a cute shirt, but it looked horrible when you tried it on. I suppose you could briefly be annoyed at the waste of time, but now you know. You leave it behind. You go out and find another shirt. This one looks really cute on you—and wah-la! You've found a winner.

In this scenario, your shopping trip was a success. So what if the first shirt (or ten) didn't look nice. Nobody cares about that. You've learned what works, and that's what matters.

When you find a winner with marketing, it's the same, but about a hundred times better.

Note about spending mistakes:

Because I care about you and feel strongly that authors should have a budget, I just want to add that you should be extra careful before jumping into any marketing with your wallet. Mistakes when it comes to spending money can obviously get very expensive, very quickly.

But if you do make mistakes with spending (and all of us have), don't wallow in what you can't fix. Instead, look for ways to make it work and/or learn from it.

That's it for now!

Thank you so much for spending time with us and reading this book. We hope that you've gained invaluable information, motivation, and encouragement about making your book the best marketing tool it can possibly be.

If you'd like to get to know us more, read our books, learn more from us, or browse the different free learning opportunities we've created for you, please check out the next two chapters "about the authors" and "resources" where we've put together a ton of information and resources to help you further between now and our next book on marketing.

Feel free to tag us!

Our social media handles are in the "About the Authors" section and you can use the hashtag #MarketingForAuthors when you share!

We can't wait to see what you do with the information in this book—if you decide to make any changes based on the advice here and you're comfortable sharing and tagging us on social media, please do! We'd love to hear about your book and your success story!

**Thank you again for reading!
If you'd like to leave a review, we'd
love to know what you think!
Sincerely, Bethany & Mandi**

THANKS FOR READING!
Please leave a short review on Amazon to let us know what you thought!

http://bit.ly/howyourbooksellsitself

MARKETING FOR AUTHORS

GROW
YOUR
AUTHOR
PLATFORM

**Generating Book Sales With Your Website,
Email Marketing, Blogging, YouTube & Pinterest
Using Content Marketing**

MANDI LYNN
WITH BETHANY ATAZADEH

PREORDER THE NEXT BOOK IN THE SERIES!

Releasing on June 4th, 2019!

"How do I get my book discovered?" It's a question every writer asks, whether it's their first book, tenth book, or if the book still needs to be published.

Every year the amount of books published grows exponentially and your story only gets lost in the shuffle. You know you should be marketing, so you start a website, maybe a newsletter or blog, but you're really just talking into the void. How do you find a place for yourself on the world wide web?

From indie authors Mandi Lynn and Bethany Atazadeh, book two in the *Marketing for Authors* series is dedicated to teaching you the many things you can do to start or grow your author platform.

Your platform is your base for all your marketing, so build it well.

Each chapter of the book is dedicated to focusing on a different platforms you can use to increase exposure for yourself and your book. We'll be talking about your website, email marketing, content marketing, search engine optimization (SEO), blogs, YouTube and Pinterest. Learn from Mandi and Bethany's personal experiences using content marketing methods to gain thousands of followers that translate into book sales.

This book is loaded with information to teach you to how to create content that shows up and that people want to share. Stop struggling to make a footprint online and instead make the web work with you.

SIGN UP FOR A RELEASE DAY EMAIL ALERT!

http://bit.ly/marketingforauthors

RESOURCES:

Here are some links from each of the chapters that we think you might find valuable!

Bethany's "Book Marketing for Authors" YouTube Playlist:

http://bit.ly/bookmarketingforauthors

Mandi's "Marketing for Authors" YouTube Playlist: http://bit.ly/2w3t3aV

Chapter 5 (The Cover)

- On Changing Book Titles and Covers (Joanna Penn from The Creative Penn)

http://bit.ly/2JtNWqP

- Cover Design by Mandi Lynn

  https://stoneridgebooks.com/book-cover-design/

Chapter 6 (The Title)

- How to Title a Book: Making Titles That Sell (Kindlepreneur)

  http://bit.ly/2UVeBOk

Chapter 7 (The Back Blurb)

- How to Create a Back Cover Blurb That Sells (Kindlepreneur)

  http://bit.ly/2TUz20X

- How to Write Back Blurb for Your Book (Joanna Penn at Creative Penn)

  http://bit.ly/2HHue8B

Chapter 8 (Taglines/Promotional Lines)

- How to Write a Tagline for Your Book and Why You Need To (Writers Helping Writers)

  http://bit.ly/2HwuisB

- What Makes a Good Tagline (Thoughts On Fantasy)

  http://bit.ly/2UOrmue

Chapter 9 (Formatting)

- Formatting 101: How to Format for Self Publishing (Bethany Atazadeh)

  http://bit.ly/2TZP3CG

- How to Format a Novel in Microsoft Word (Mandi Lynn)

  http://bit.ly/2uiz58c

- DIY Book Formats

  https://diybookformats.com/

- How to Format Your Self Published Book (Moira Allen)

  http://bit.ly/2CxN3rd

- Interior Book Design and Formatting (Book Baby)

  http://bit.ly/2JwPMqQ

Chapter 10 (Editors)

- Looking for a Professional Book Editor (Reedsy)

  http://bit.ly/2TWNeXf

- Goodreads: Editors and Writers Group
  http://bit.ly/2TjZVXG

Chapter 11 and 12 (Keywords and Categories)

- Make Your Book More Discoverable with Keywords (Kindle Direct Publishing)
  https://amzn.to/2W8qTDs
- How to Choose the Right Keywords (Kindlepreneur)
  http://bit.ly/2OkbflF
- Optimizing Your Books for Amazon Keyword Search (Jane Friedman)
  http://bit.ly/2FeeG9e
- Choosing the Right Categories and Keywords for Your Book (The Creative Penn)
  http://bit.ly/2Tt5vHq
- How to Get Approved for More Amazon Book Categories (Self Publishing School)
  http://bit.ly/2TOHuj2
- 3 Tools for Amazon Keyword Research in 2018
  http://bit.ly/2TNVF7X

- Secret Method to Choosing Amazon Book Categories in KDP

  http://bit.ly/2OhPmU1

ABOUT THE AUTHORS

Bethany's Book Marketing Journey:

For me personally, I used Instagram as my first marketing platform. I got the word out there by talking about my book and being excited about it, which in turn helped others to begin talking about it. I made it searchable by using hashtags.

I also focused on book reviews (both on Amazon as well as reviews on the Instagram platform itself), by reaching out to readers directly on Instagram and connecting with them to see if they'd like to review my book.

My second marketing platform quickly became YouTube, as I joined what is often called the "AuthorTube" community. YouTube is actually considered a search engine, so every time I post about a searchable topic and make sure to include my book in the video, I am marketing my work. It is also a valid word of mouth tool, since other writers and readers often tell their friends about my channel and/or books.

Besides marketing via Instagram and YouTube, I have tried many other marketing techniques (some that I still do to this day), such as my newsletter,

Facebook ads and Amazon ads, guest posting, book signings, and so on.

I've learned a LOT in my time as a self-published author, but my biggest lessons that I hope I have imparted well within these pages is that you're only one person. You can't do everything. But you *can* accomplish quite a bit, if you focus on the right tools. Especially if one of those tools is your book.

Mandi's Book Marketing Journey:

My journey of book marketing started on YouTube when I was documenting my journey of being an author. This was back in 2012 when there weren't many authors on YouTube and the term "AuthorTube" had yet to be coined.

Over time I went from talking about my journey of becoming an author, to teaching others how to write and publish their novels.

I made myself known in the community and when I finally published my book, I had an eager audience ready to read.

After graduating from college I became more focused on my digital marketing platform and extending my reach across most social media networks such as Instagram, Twitter, Facebook and Pinterest.

Today I work full time in content marketing and use my skills towards my own digital marketing strategies as well as work with other authors to coach them in building their platforms.

When it comes to reaching your readers, I learned very quickly that you must take advantage of every opportunity you get.

When people ask what you do, you tell them you write books. When you're at a book convention, try to, at the least, get people to walk away with your business card and sign up for your newsletter.

Marketing is all about taking advantage of every opportunity possible.

ABOUT: BETHANY

Bethany Atazadeh is a Minnesota-based author of *Evalene's Number, Pearl's Number, The Confident Corgi, Penny's Puppy Pack for Writers,* and now *How Your Book Sells Itself.* She graduated from Northwestern College in 2008 with a Bachelor of Arts degree in English with a writing emphasis. After graduation, she pursued songwriting, recording, and performing with her band, and writing was no longer a priority. But in 2016, she was inspired by the NaNoWriMo challenge to write a novel in 30 days, and since then she hasn't stopped. She is passionate about God, her husband, writing, music, and dogs, specifically her Corgi puppy, Penny.

BOOKS BY BETHANY

 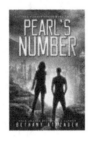 

CONNECT WITH BETHANY ON:

Website: www.bethanyatazadeh.com

Instagram: @authorbethanyatazadeh

Facebook: @authorbethanyatazadeh

Twitter: @bethanyatazadeh

YouTube: www.youtube.com/bethanyatazadeh

Goodreads: Bethany Atazadeh

Patreon: www.patreon.com/bethanyatazadeh

ABOUT: MANDI

 *Mandi Lynn* published her first novel when she was seventeen. The author of *Essence*, *I am Mercy* and *She's Not Here*, Mandi spends her days continuing to write and creating YouTube videos to help other writers achieve their dreams of seeing their books published. Mandi is the owner of Stone Ridge Books, a company that works to help authors bring their books to life through cover design and digital book marketing. She is also the creator of AuthorTube Academy, a course that teaches authors how to grow their presence on YouTube and find loyal readers.

When she's not creating, you can find Mandi exploring her backyard or getting lost in the woods.

BOOKS BY MANDI:

 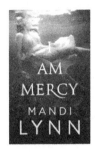 

CONNECT WITH MANDI ON:

Website: https://mandilynn.com

Instagram: @mandilynnwrites

Facebook: @mandilynnwrites

Twitter: @mandilynnwrites

YouTube: www.youtube.com/mandilynnVLOGS

Goodreads: Mandi Lynn

AuthorTube Academy: bit.ly/AuthorTubeAcademy

AuthorTube Academy Facebook Group:

http://bit.ly/2JhamHY

Mandi's Patreon: http://bit.ly/2NnhXa6

Made in the USA
Las Vegas, NV
05 February 2025

17584046R00105